Will I Be a Rock Star?

Written by Cynthia Stierle
Based on the series created by Michael Poryes and Rich Correll & Barry O'Brien

Ask me anything!

Reader's Digest
Children's Books®

Pleasantville, New York • Montréal, Québec • Bath, United Kingdom

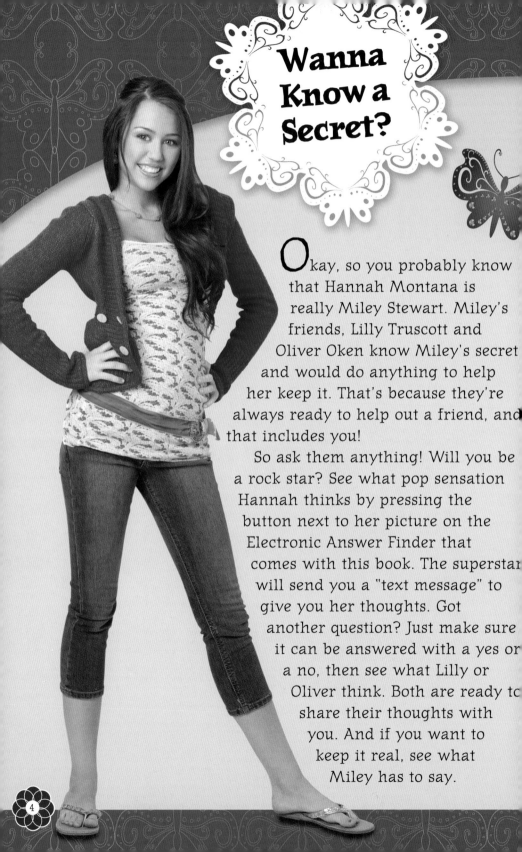

Wanna Know a Secret?

Okay, so you probably know that Hannah Montana is really Miley Stewart. Miley's friends, Lilly Truscott and Oliver Oken know Miley's secret and would do anything to help her keep it. That's because they're always ready to help out a friend, and that includes you!

So ask them anything! Will you be a rock star? See what pop sensation Hannah thinks by pressing the button next to her picture on the Electronic Answer Finder that comes with this book. The superstar will send you a "text message" to give you her thoughts. Got another question? Just make sure it can be answered with a yes or a no, then see what Lilly or Oliver think. Both are ready to share their thoughts with you. And if you want to keep it real, see what Miley has to say.

Oliver

Lilly

t's fun to imagine all the
ossibilities—who knows what
ou might grow up to be?

With so many questions, where
hould you start? The answer to that
s easy—in this book of course. It's
illed with questions and quizzes
hat might help you see who you are
nd who you'd like to be. If you're
retty sure of your answers, you
on't need to check in with Hannah
nd company. But if you don't know
r just want to see what someone
lse thinks, then just use the
lectronic Answer Finder. It might
e fun to take a quiz twice and
ompare answers.

Just keep in mind that the key
vord is "fun." If you think
lannah might not have it right,
ust ask your question again.
fter all, even part-time pop
tars aren't perfect. Everybody
nakes mistakes!

LET'S ALL HANG OUT

Miley, Lilly, and Oliver like to chil-lax at the beach, even if they do have to put up with Rico and pay for overpriced water at his surf shack. While the beach is great, it's not the only place to have fun. Answer the questions to see where you and your friends might want to go when you've got some downtime. Then check in with Miley and the gang and see where they'd like to go to kick back.

1 If you're hanging out and want to get food, you'd want to:
- check out the selection at the food court.
- check out the selection in the refrigerator.
- see if you can spot a pushcart vendor or snack shack.

2 To listen to some tunes together, you and your friends:
- check out the cool clothing stores where the music is blasting.
- play the latest downloads on your computer.
- head to the park with your iPods and share playlists.

3 You and your BFF want the sun-kissed look for an upcoming dance, so you:
- go to the tanning boutique for a spray-on experience.
- do the self-tanning thing in your room.
- already have the look, since you're both outdoors all the time.

4 You and your friends love to:
- browse through the stores.
- make YouTube videos or play video games.
- get a game going—beach volleyball, Frisbee, whatever.

5 If you need to take a break, you and your friends:
- sit in the massage chairs at the gadget store.
- watch TV.
- sit under a shady tree and drink some water.

6 For your birthday it would be great if the 'rents got you:

- 🚗 gift cards to your fave stores.
- 🚗 a Foosball table.
- 🚗 a mountain bike.

7 You'd like to be in a place where you could:

- 🚗 see and be seen.
- 🚗 have privacy.
- 🚗 get some fresh air.

8 There's nothing you need to dress for, so you wear:

- 🚗 your latest purchases.
- 🚗 loungewear.
- 🚗 whatever the weather calls for.

SCORING:

MOSTLY 🚗'S: The Mall. You and your friends like to shop till you drop, then you'll refuel at the food court. And it's always fun to see who you'll meet on the weekends.

MOSTLY 🚗'S: Home Sweet Home. You and your friends like to hang out at each other's houses. You can just be yourselves, with all the comforts of home.

MOSTLY 🚗'S: Park It. You and your friends like to play wherever you can, so you're likely to want to hang out at a public park. It might be a beach, a skating rink, or a grassy playing field, as long as you can all join in the fun.

CALLING ALL CRUSHES

Would you rather go to the mall or check out the cute guys at the beach? That's an easy question for Miley and Lilly. (BTW the answer is: see the cute guys at the beach.) It's fun to crush on people. But who's the right crush for you? A sweet and sensitive guy or a guy that has you ROFL? Take the quiz, then check your score with Lilly or Miley or both to see if they agree.

1. You'd love it if your crush sent you a funny Valentine that made you laugh.
   YES — that would be perfect.
   MAYBE — whatever he picked would be fine—as long as it's from him.
   NO — you'd want something a little more romantic.

2. You'd love it if your crush sent texts with the joke of the day.
   YES — even the lame ones are worth a chuckle.
   MAYBE — if he thought they were really funny.
   NO — you'd rather have more personal messages.

3. When you're walking down the hallways together, you and your crush are always laughing.
   YES — he cracks you up.
   MAYBE — if you're both in a good mood.
   NO — you're too busy gazing into each other's eyes.

4. You're walking by a kids' playground and your crush wants to go on the swings. Do you go with him?
   YES — you'll challenge him to see who can swing higher.
   MAYBE — if you feel like it, but it's okay if you don't.
   NO — only if there's a swing for two.

5. Your crush does a cannonball into the pool and soaks you on purpose. Do you laugh?
   YES — he's just being playful.
   MAYBE — as long as you were going in, anyway.
   NO — in fact, it would really bother you.

6. You'd love to stroll, hand in hand, through a carnival.
   YES — you'd both have fun playing the games and
             going on rides.
   MAYBE — as long as you'd be together.
   NO — you'd rather be someplace quiet where you can talk.

7. You're at a party that's kind of dull, so the host breaks out a karaoke machine. Your crush wants to be the first one to give it a shot, even though he can't sing. Do you encourage him?

    YES — it would be worth it to liven up the party.

    MAYBE — if he can turn it into a group sing-along.

    NO — you wouldn't want him to be embarrassed.

8. Your crush has to write a poem for English class. Would he turn in this silly rhyme?

I'm not a poet, don't tell me, I know it.

It's because I'm not very good, picking words like I should.

When your favorite color is purple, it's . . . kind of a problem.

    YES — he'd do it as a joke.

    MAYBE — you *think* the English teacher has a sense of humor.

    NO — he'd take the assignment seriously.

SCORING:

YES = 1 point

MAYBE = 2 points

NO = 3 points

8—13:
COMIC CUTIE.
Your crush is a guy that keeps you laughing. You're full of smiles for him.

14—19
FRIENDLY & FUN.
Your crush is someone who's fun, but he's also aware of other people. His down-to-earth style is right up your alley.

20—24:
ROMANTIC ROMEO.
Your crush is sweet, considerate, and more on the serious side. That's fine by you.

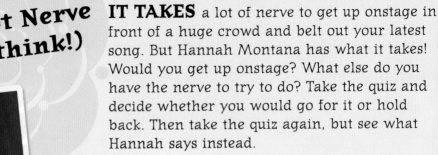

I Got Nerve (I think!)

IT TAKES a lot of nerve to get up onstage in front of a huge crowd and belt out your latest song. But Hannah Montana has what it takes! Would you get up onstage? What else do you have the nerve to try to do? Take the quiz and decide whether you would go for it or hold back. Then take the quiz again, but see what Hannah says instead.

1. Your school PTA is sponsoring an art contest. The winning entry will go on to a national contest. Do you submit your drawings even though you've never shown them to anybody before?

2. A cute new guy just transferred to your school—and he's in your class. Not only that, but he happens to sit right behind you in homeroom. Do you offer to show him around?

3. The community youth program is sponsoring a talent show. A friend wants to pull together a girl band. She wants everyone to dress up, dance, and lip-synch your favorite song. Do you join the band?

4. You never learned to ice-skate, but a friend is having a birthday party at a local ice arena. Your crush is going. Do you go to the party, too—even though your crush will see you clumsily clinging to the rink walls instead of gracefully gliding across the ice?

5. You hear one of the more popular girls in school gossiping about a good friend—and the rumor she's spreading is totally untrue. Do you speak up?

6. The auditions for the school play are next week. You've always wanted to try acting, but you know the drama teacher can be really tough. It might be a great learning experience, or a totally embarrassing one. Do you sign up?

7. You didn't make the travel soccer team last year. It's tryout time again. There are some openings on the team, but you know the rest of the players are really competitive. Do you try out?

8. Your neighbor is planning a fashion show as a charity fund-raiser. She asks you to be one of the models for the show, which will take place at the mall. Your neighbor mentions to your parents that she'll be choosing all the clothes herself. It's fine with your parents, but you have serious questions about your neighbor's sense of style. Do you agree to do it, anyway?

9. You have a great voice, and your principal wants you to sing the national anthem at the next school assembly. You've never sung in public before. Do you make your debut?

10. You love to make jewelry. All your friends love your pieces, and one offers to take some pictures and help you create a brochure to showcase your talent. Is it time to launch your own business?

HANNAH:

There are no right or wrong answers here— you need to do what you're comfortable doing.

If you answered "yes" *to most of these questions, then you've got nerves of steel! New experiences excite you. Even if everything doesn't work out exactly as planned, that doesn't stop you from trying again next time.*

If you answered "no" *to most of these questions, then you like to stay on the safe side of things. That's fine, but don't be afraid to take a chance now and again. You'll probably surprise yourself when you see what you can really do!*

If you answered with a mix of "yes" and "no" or even "I don't know," *then you're ready to dive in when you think the reward is worth the risk. You know what's right for you, so follow your head and your heart!*

G.N.I. (GIRLS' NIGHT IN)

IT'S A girls' night out—in your house. After all, staying in can be as much fun as going out. You invite your best buds over to spend the night, but what should you plan to do? Follow the path to see which sleepover will keep everyone from falling asleep—then see if Lilly and Miley agree with the direction you're heading in.

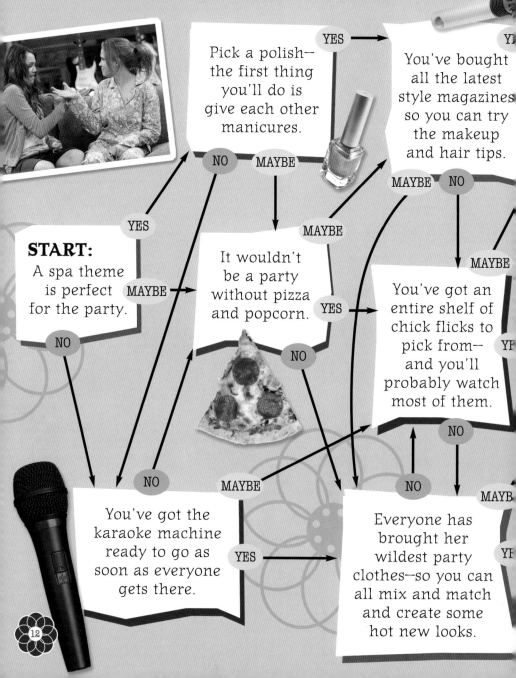

Pick a polish—
the first thing
you'll do is
give each other
manicures.

YES

You've bought
all the latest
style magazines
so you can try
the makeup
and hair tips.

Y

NO   **MAYBE**

MAYBE   **NO**

YES

MAYBE

START:
A spa theme
is perfect
for the party.

MAYBE

It wouldn't
be a party
without pizza
and popcorn.

MAYBE

MAYBE

You've got an
entire shelf of
chick flicks to
pick from—
and you'll
probably watch
most of them.

YES

NO

YP

NO

NO

NO

MAYBE

NO

MAYBE

You've got the
karaoke machine
ready to go as
soon as everyone
gets there.

YES

Everyone has
brought her
wildest party
clothes—so you can
all mix and match
and create some
hot new looks.

YP

MAYB

12

It's a hairy-scary experience when everyone has her hair in rollers and face slathered in skin cream—so you take pictures!

YES →

MAYBE NO

PAMPERING PARTY.
Break out the nail polish, hairbrushes, and lipsticks! This party is all about making you and your friends look and feel good.

NO

You'll all be drama queens as you act out the scenes.

YES →

MAYBE

FOOD AND FLICKS. What can be more fun than watching a movie and eating popcorn in your pj's with all your BFFs around to enjoy the experience with you?

MAYBE

NO

Your friends show off their best moves as the music blares—and you make a great music video!

YES →

DANCING DIVAS. It's time to get a little crazy— right in your own house. You and your fellow pop stars can dress up in your wildest clothes and dance the night away.

ON THE (AMAZING) ROAD AGAIN

All aboard! Hannah Montana is hitting the road and going on a concert tour! One of the cool benefits of being a pop star is getting to travel around and see new places. But if you were kicking off your concert tour, where would you start? Since your fans everywhere are great, you can decide based on what else you can see while you're there! Then see if Hannah is okay with double billing as you start your tour together.

1. You would love to have tea:
  A. with the queen.
  B. in the Russian Tea Room.
  C. in a special ceremony.

2. It would be amazing to get tickets to see:
  A. a football game at Wembley Stadium.
  B. a basketball game at Madison Square Garden.
  C. a baseball game at the Tokyo Dome.

3. You're in a seafood mood, so for lunch you'd like to try:
  A. fish and chips.
  B. lox and bagels.
  C. sushi.

4. You'd be most excited by the neon lights of:
  A. Piccadilly Circus.
  B. Times Square.
  C. Shibuya.

5. For fresh air and exercise, you'd like to walk around:
  A. Kensington Gardens.
  B. Central Park.
  C. Imperial Palace Gardens.

HANNAH SAYS: It really doesn't matter where you start—I had never heard of half of these places until I looked them up on the Internet. And I learned that each city is special in its own way—so I plan to visit them all!

6. You can't wait to take pictures from the top of:
   A. the London Eye.
   B. the Empire State Building.
   C. Tokyo Tower.

7. If you were feeling reflective you'd visit:
   A. Westminster Abbey.
   B. Saint Patrick's Cathedral.
   C. Asakusa Kannon Temple.

8. You'd really like to spend some time window shopping:
   A. as you walk down Oxford Street.
   B. as you stroll down Fifth Avenue.
   C. as you amble through the Ginza Shopping District.

MOSTLY A's:
Cheerio! London, England, is the place where you can start your tour!

MOSTLY B's:
Begin your tour in the Big Apple, New York City! And give your regards to Broadway.

MOSTLY C's:
Visit the land of the rising sun and start your concert tour in Toyko, Japan. *Sayonara!*

WORKIN' FOR A LIVIN'

Working for Rico is no day at the beach—just ask Jackson. So maybe it's time for him to look for a new job. But what about you? If you wanted to make some extra cash over the summer, what kind of job would be right for you? Check with Jackson's business partner in the cheeze-jerky business, Oliver, to see if you're on the road to riches, or will at least make enough money to go to the movies.

1. Your friends always admire how clean and neat your locker looks.
   YES — you hate clutter.
   MAYBE — it's not always neat, but it's always decorated.
   NO — you don't mind a little mess.

2. The folders you use in school are color-coded for each subject.
   YES — it makes it easy to find the one you need
   MAYBE — you've doodled a lot on them, so it's hard to tell.
   NO — but you manage, anyway.

3. You have no problem chatting with teachers and coaches.
   YES — you actually like talking to adults.
   MAYBE — you'd rather talk to kids your own age.
   NO — but you're great with little kids.

4. You don't mind being in one place all day.
   YES — as long as your mind is busy, you're happy.
   MAYBE — you'd need to move around a little bit.
   NO — you'd need to move around a lot.

5. You plan to make your holiday wish list a PowerPoint presentation.
   YES — everyone will appreciate how easy it is to understand.
   MAYBE — if it turns into a fashion slide show.
   NO — you like to do these things by hand.

6. You don't mind wearing dress clothes every day.

YES — dressing up is fun.

MAYBE — as long as the clothing can be cutting edge, too.

NO — you'd rather be in a T-shirt and shorts in the summer.

7. Your room has lots of organized shelves.

YES — it's great to have your stuff at your fingertips.

MAYBE — the baskets are overflowing with accessories.

NO — there are more arts and crafts scattered everywhere than anything else.

8. When your friends send you pictures, you download and sort the pics into e-scrapbooks.

YES — you print out the pages and impress everyone.

MAYBE — you use the pages to decorate your closet door.

NO — you just print out the pics and make your own frames.

SCORING: 1 point for every YES, 2 points for every MAYBE, and 3 points for every NO.

If your score was between 8 and 12, you're an OFFICE ORGANIZER! The boss would love your ease with computers, your organizational skills, and your professional manner.

If your score was between 13 and 18, you're a BOUTIQUE BABE! Shoppers would flock to you for tips on the latest styles and the latest sales.

If your score was between 19 and 24, you'd make a GREAT CAMP COUNSELOR! Working with younger kids doing arts and crafts, outdoor activities, and generally having fun would make work a pleasure.

I've Got a Secret

(Secret Celebrity / Part-time Pop Star)

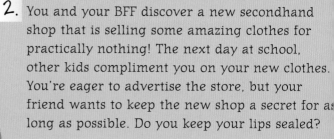

Miley knows she can count on Lilly and Oliver not to tell anyone that she's Hannah Montana. But how well can you keep a secret? Find out if you're as trusty as a vault or as open as a 24-hour convenience store! Then ask Oliver and Lilly whether they think you can do what you say.

1. Your friend got an ugly sweater for her birthday from an aunt who lives far away. You know this friend also happens to be short on cash, but you're surprised to see her give the sweater to someone else as a gift. Do you spill to the new owner of the ugly sweater?

2. You and your BFF discover a new secondhand shop that is selling some amazing clothes for practically nothing! The next day at school, other kids compliment you on your new clothes. You're eager to advertise the store, but your friend wants to keep the new shop a secret for as long as possible. Do you keep your lips sealed?

3. You know two of your friends are crushing on the same guy. He asks one of them to go out, and she accepts. But she wants to be the one to break the news to your other friend after school. Do you text the other friend before then?

4. Your friend split her jeans! She's draped a hoodie around her waist, so she's covered. But you keep cracking up! (It is funny—even your friend admits it.) Do you let a few people in on the "cover-up"?

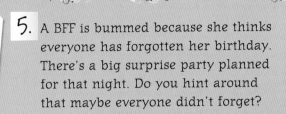

5. A BFF is bummed because she thinks everyone has forgotten her birthday. There's a big surprise party planned for that night. Do you hint around that maybe everyone didn't forget?

6. You and your friends go to a pool party. A friend says she doesn't want to go into the water because it's too cold, but you know it's because she can't swim. Do you tell everyone and hand her a pair of Floaties?

7. You saw an awesome movie over the weekend—it was full of suspense and the ending had a great twist. You want to talk about it at school, but one of your friends hasn't seen the film yet. Do you talk about it, anyway?

8. You know where your parents have hidden your brother's birthday present. His birthday is tomorrow, but he's dying to know if they bought him an Xbox 360. He swears he'll act surprised when he opens the present, no matter what. Do you reveal the location of the loot?

Score 1 point for every **YES** answer, then tally your points and see how you rate as a keeper of secrets.

0-2: You are a locked vault—so any secret is pretty safe with you!

3-5: You have some secret slips. Sometimes you can manage to keep a secret in . . . and sometimes you can't.

6-8: You're an open book. When you've got news, it's just too hard to keep it in.

GET THE PARTY PUMPIN'

Hannah likes all kinds of music—not just her own! And she loves to dance. What kind of music gets your body pumpin'? And when you move to the music, what kinds of dancing do you enjoy most? Then see what Hannah thinks about your dancing—maybe you're ready to be one of her backup dancers!

1. To you "put on your dancing shoes" means:

- grabbing ballet slippers or taps.
- lacing up your favorite sneakers.
- putting on a pair of pretty heels.

2. You like it when the crowd:

- applauds your performance.
- makes room for you and your partner to glide across the floor.
- is dancing along with you.

3. You'd like to wear a dance costume made from:

- satin and tulle.
- silk and sequins.
- the clothes in your closet.

4. If you get thirsty after dancing you'll want to sip:

- spring water with a slice of lemon.
- fruit punch with two straws.
- an energy drink.

5. You think it would be fun to:

- go on a national tour with a dance company.
- take part in a ballroom dance competition on TV.
- make a music video with your fave R & B artist.

6. As you move to the music you feel:

- beautiful.
- fiery.
- energized.

7. The musical instruments you listen for are:

- violins and flutes.
- the brass section.
- drums and the bass.

There are LOTS of different styles of dancing. There are also different ethnic dances, like belly dancing, hula dancing, or Irish step dancing. So take a chance and DANCE however, wherever, and whenever you can!

8. When others watch you dance, they'll be blown away by your:

- gracefulness.
- fancy footwork.
- creativity.

MOSTLY ⁆'S : **Stage Style.** Whether it's ballet, tap, or jazz, you feel good performing onstage in front of an audience.

MOSTLY ⁆'S : **It Takes Two.** From ballroom and swing dancing to some south-of-the-border sizzle with salsa dancing, your favorite moves are with a partner.

MOSTLY ⁆'S : **Dance Club Dazzle.** From hip-hop moves to popping and locking, you've got the rhythm of the street moving through your feet.

P-A-R-T-Y

Hannah Montana gets invited to some great parties, so she has met lots of celebrities! But a party doesn't have to be star-studded to be a lot of fun. Why not think about hosting a party of your own? What kind of party should you throw?

No one knows more about parties than Oliver. (At least, he thinks he does.) So check to see if Oliver agrees with your choices—if not, see what kind of par-tay the O-man picks for you.

1. To get everyone the party 411, you would:
- **a.** mail engraved invitations.
- **b.** send a text.
- **c.** make flyers with all the details and hand them out. The more the merrier.

2. To answer the big pre-party question, "What should I wear?" you'd tell people:
- **a.** wear something elegant.
- **b.** wear something funky.
- **c.** wear something comfortable.

3. When a guest arrives, he or she might want to try:
- **a.** one of the fancy appetizers.
- **b.** the spicy salsa and chips.
- **c.** a hamburger or salad.

4. The perfect setting for your dream party would be:
- **a.** a lavish yacht.
- **b.** a big dance floor with a disco ball.
- **c.** a big beach house with an outdoor patio.

5. Every party needs music, so you'd hire:
- **a.** a string quartet or a pianist.
- **b.** an MC and a DJ.
- **c.** a band that rocks.

6. Your guests would arrive:
- **a.** in limousines.
- **b.** in cars or taxis.
- **c.** whatever, as long as they get there.

MOSTLY A'S:
Your fantasy party would be an elegant event, complete with ice sculptures, designer dresses, and an A-list guest list.

MOSTLY B'S:
Your dream would be to host a happening dance party that got all of your guests moving their feet to the beat.

MOSTLY C'S:
You'd hope to have a huge blowout with as many people as possible! It would be casual but lots of fun!